A Visit to PAKISTAN

by Charis Mather

Minneapolis, Minnesota

Credits

All images are courtesy of Shutterstock.com, unless otherwise specified. With thanks to Getty Images, Thinkstock Photo, and iStockphoto.

Cover – thsulemani, Wit.Siri, kavram. 2 – Aaliyah Kha. 4-5 – Arfan Mahmood, ixpert. 6-7 – nortongo, Umer Arif. 8-9 – Burhan Ay Photography. 10-11 – Aqib Yasin, Sun_Shine. 12-13 – SooperChef Studios, Charoen Krung Photography, small1. 14-15 – TripDeeDee Photo, Jawwad Ali. 16-17 – Pawika Tongtavee, Sulo Letta. 18-19 – Armensl, Kamal Hari Menon. 20-21 – Burhan Ay Photography, Jrs Jahangeer. 22-23 – Farris Noorzali, khlongwangchao.

Library of Congress Cataloging-in-Publication Data is available at www.loc.gov or upon request from the publisher.

ISBN: 979-8-88509-376-7 (hardcover)
ISBN: 979-8-88509-498-6 (paperback)
ISBN: 979-8-88509-613-3 (ebook)

© 2023 Booklife Publishing
This edition is published by arrangement with Booklife Publishing.

North American adaptations © 2023 Bearport Publishing Company. All rights reserved. No part of this publication may be reproduced in whole or in part, stored in any retrieval system, or transmitted in any form or by any means, electronic, mechanical, photocopying, recording, or otherwise, without written permission from the publisher.

For more information, write to Bearport Publishing, 5357 Penn Avenue South, Minneapolis, MN 55419.

CONTENTS

Country to Country 4
Today's Trip Is to Pakistan! 6
Lahore 8
Bazaars 10
Food and Drinks 12
Mohenjo-daro 14
Karakoram Highway 16
Animals 18
Khewra Salt Mine 20
Before You Go 22
Glossary 24
Index 24

COUNTRY TO COUNTRY

A country is an area of land marked by **borders**. The people in each country have their own rules and ways of living. They may speak different languages.

Which country do you live in?

Each country around the world has its own interesting things to see and do. Let's take a trip to visit a country and learn more!

Have you ever visited another country?

TODAY'S TRIP IS TO
PAKISTAN!

Pakistan is a country in the **continent** of Asia.

FACT FILE

Capital city: Islamabad
Main languages: Urdu and English
Currency: Pakistani rupee
Flag:

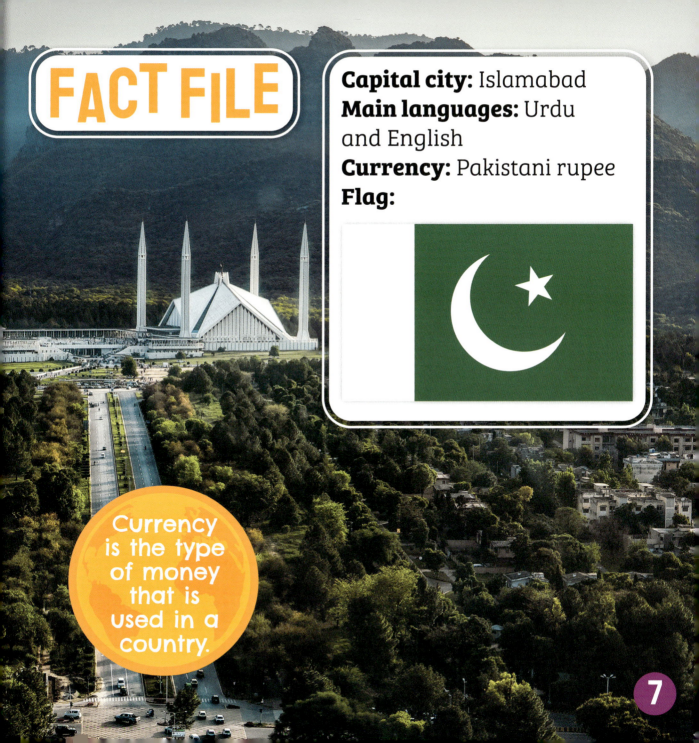

Currency is the type of money that is used in a country.

7

LAHORE

We'll start our trip in one of Pakistan's biggest cities, Lahore. The city is known for its old buildings, including Lahore Fort. People visit this huge structure to learn about the country's history.

8

Not far from the fort is Badshahi **Mosque**. This huge, red building is one of the many beautiful mosques in Pakistan.

BAZAARS

Many cities and towns in Pakistan have **traditional** markets called bazaars. People can buy all kinds of things at these lively markets.

Bazaars are full of little shops. Some sell colorful carpets or clothes, while others have art or handmade pots. Bazaars are a good place to find Pakistani food, too.

FOOD AND DRINKS

One popular dish in Pakistan is a meat stew called *nihari*. It is cooked very slowly. Sometimes, people eat *nihari* for breakfast after letting it cook all night!

If you're thirsty, try some sugarcane juice. This popular drink tastes best right after it is squeezed from the sweet plant.

Sugarcane

Sugarcane juice is made and sold by some **street vendors**.

MOHENJO-DARO

Next, we'll go see **ruins** of the ancient city Mohenjo-daro. This city was built thousands of years ago. **Archaeologists** believe at least 35,000 people lived there.

14

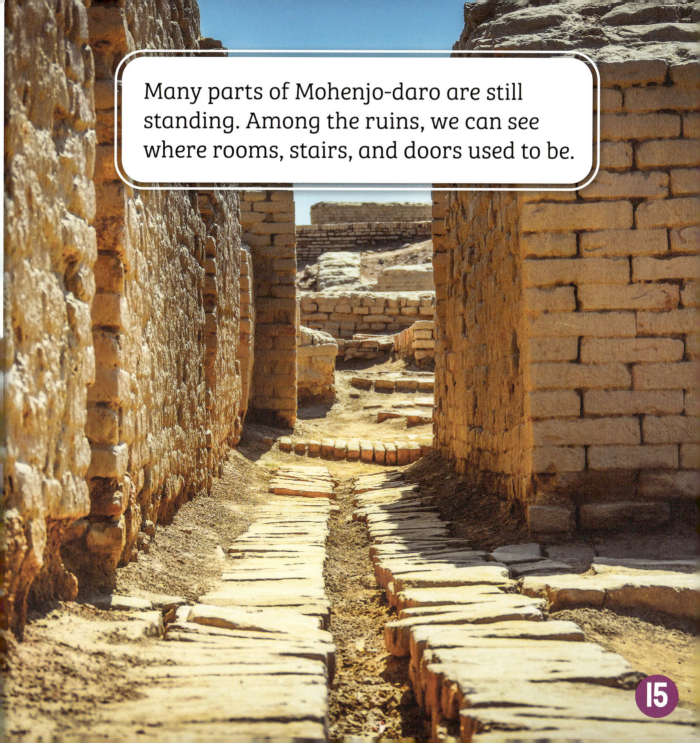

Many parts of Mohenjo-daro are still standing. Among the ruins, we can see where rooms, stairs, and doors used to be.

KARAKORAM HIGHWAY

The Karakoram Highway is also called the China-Pakistan Friendship Highway.

Let's take a drive on the Karakoram Highway. This road winds through the Karakoram Mountains, which have some of the world's highest **peaks**. Parts of the road are more than 15,000 feet (4,500 m) high.

We'll have to drive carefully. There are some spots where the road is very narrow and can fit only one car at a time.

ANIMALS

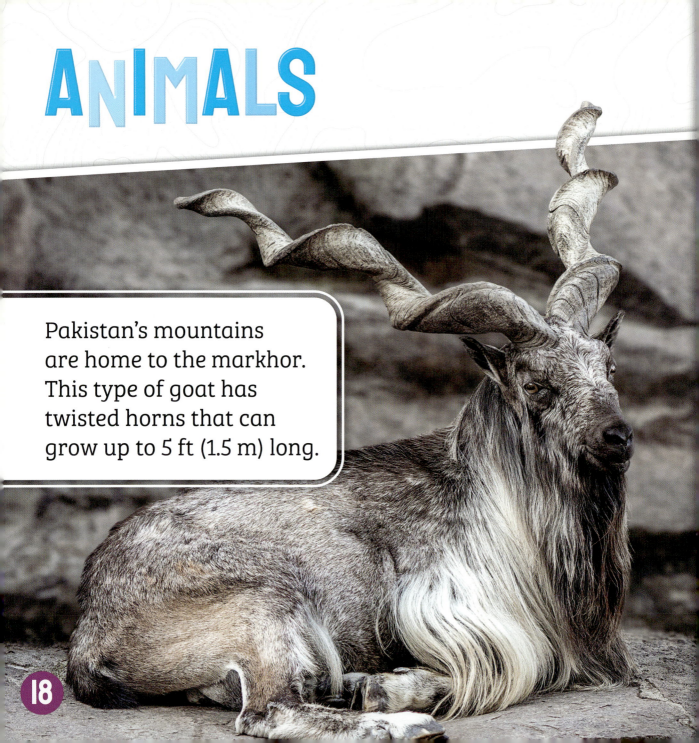

Pakistan's mountains are home to the markhor. This type of goat has twisted horns that can grow up to 5 ft (1.5 m) long.

We might also see some chukar partridges.
These birds have red beaks and striped wings.
People in Pakistan believe they are a sign of love.

KHEWRA SALT MINE

Pakistan has one of the world's biggest salt **mines**. The Khewra Salt Mine was discovered more than 2,000 years ago when an ancient Greek king saw his horses licking salty rocks.

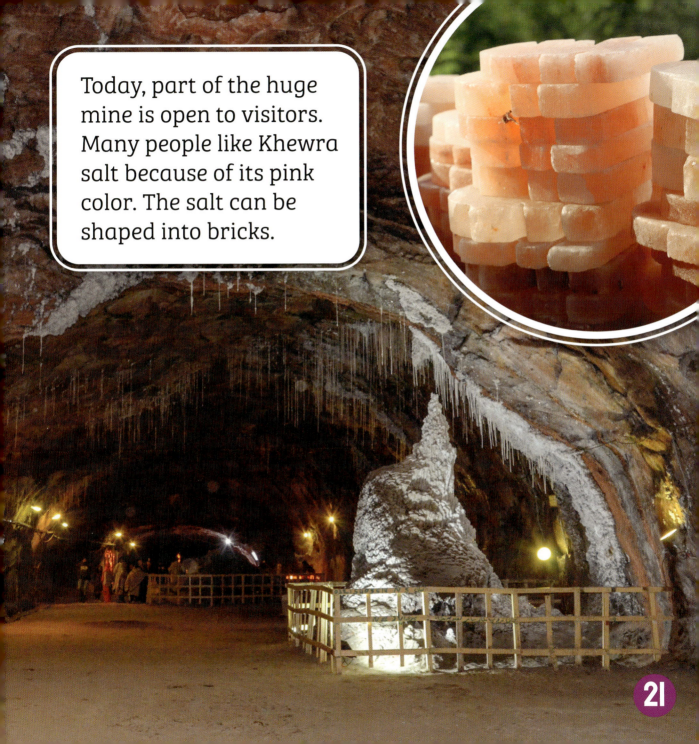

Today, part of the huge mine is open to visitors. Many people like Khewra salt because of its pink color. The salt can be shaped into bricks.

BEFORE YOU GO

We can't forget to see Attabad Lake, found in a part of Pakistan called the Hunza Valley. This lake formed in 2010 after a **landslide** blocked a river.

Attabad Lake

Attabad Lake is surrounded by mountains. The entire valley has beautiful things to see all year long.

What have you learned about Pakistan on this trip?

Hunza Valley

GLOSSARY

archaeologists scientists who learn about ancient times by studying things they dig up, such as old buildings

borders lines that show where one place ends and another begins

continent one of the world's seven large land masses

landslide a natural disaster where the land in an area has fallen into another area

mines underground tunnels people have made to get to valuable things that are in the ground

mosque a building where people who follow the religion Islam go to worship

peaks the tops of mountains

ruins parts of buildings or structures that are still left after a long time has passed

street vendors people who sell things along the sides of roads

traditional relating to something that a group of people has done for many years

INDEX

bazaars 10–11
cities 7–8, 10, 14–15
food 11–12
goats 18
mosques 9
mountains 16, 18, 23
partridges 19
ruins 14–15
salt 20–21